The Paper Diet

What you gain by reducing excess paper

D0061893

Kater Leatherman

Kater Leatherman

Cover design by
Kater Leatherman

Author photograph on the back
by Penny Lane Lifestyle Photography

Formatting by Candace Nikiforou

Kiwi Publishing
First printing, September 2016

ISBN: 978-0-9786136-3-1

Note: This book is written as a source of information,
not a substitute for professional advice.
Please search the internet for answers
to questions that aren't in this book.
I have purposely not listed specific web sites
as they sometimes expire or change.

Note that "die" is in the word "diet".
Die means to leave behind.
Going on a paper diet is not just about reducing
clutter but letting go of anything
that is keeping you from being
happy, healthy and whole.

FACT:

*The average American spends one year
of their life looking for misplaced items.*

FACT:

*Eighty percent of the paper we keep
is never accessed again.*

FACT:

*Every year, the average American
receives about 41 pounds of junk mail;
approximately 44% of it ends up
in our landfills unopened.*

Introduction

With all the clutter in our lives, the one that we most struggle with is paper. One reason is that so much more comes in than goes out. Every day, we are bombarded with it - through the mail, being out in the world (shopping receipts, advertising flyers, take out menus) and from our family members who bring paper home from school and/or work.

It's a quandary like none other. And then there are the stakes, which feel much higher with paper than possessions. What if we can't return something without a receipt? What if we get audited and the IRS needs supporting information that we've misplaced or tossed? What if we get rid of a document that we might need for legal reasons? It's the "what ifs" that cause us to keep so much paper.

Whether you think that every piece of paper has significance and can't be replaced... or you don't know where to put it or how to set up a filing system... or you can't figure out what to keep and what to toss out, this simple book is your guide to help reduce your paper piles and keep them under control, once and for all.

But wait... this is not just another how to book. The Paper Diet also addresses why we choose to keep paper, the payoffs for holding on to it and what prevents us from moving forward. You will gain the tools necessary to keep going when you hit that plateau and want to give up. In other words, while you're reducing volume, creating s p a c e, and getting organized, you are also on a path of self-discovery. After all, is it not a known fact that we are our clutter?

So now you've taken the first step. Keep reading. Do something every day that moves you in the direction of living with less paper. With time and patience, the journey from too much to just enough will reflect a desire for balance, clarity, energy, insight and s p a c e in your one very precious life!

– Kater Leatherman

The Paper Diet's definition of "just enough":
choosing to keep paper that is either sentimental,
useful, needed, loved or wanted.
Optional: paper that has monetary worth.

Contents

Clutter, like fat, insulates us from the world around us.
Paper piles become barriers that we hide behind
to shield our pain. By dismantling the walls that keep you
from having the life that you want,
you are learning to get comfortable
with being uncomfortable.
Change happens when we are able to tolerate and
move through discomfort.

10 benefits of reducing excess paper

It will free your energy to focus on other things.

With less to take care of,
you will feel energetically lighter.

You will have more time to slow down and enjoy life.

As your attachment to paper diminishes,
you will have less tolerance for all types of clutter.

It will raise your inner awareness.

You will save time and stress by giving up the
hide and seek game where you are either avoiding
or always looking for things.

The more you get used to letting go,
the easier it will be to let go.

You will be creating s p a c e for something new,
better and/or different to come into your life.

You will feel more inner abundance.

You will live your life with clarity, truth and integrity
rather than fear, evasion and distraction.

We all come hard wired with something.
Some of us are highly sensitive people.
Others are born with the depression gene
or prone to addictive behaviors.
Still others are just better at adapting to change.
But what if you are someone who is hard wired
for being loss adverse?
What if the loss that comes with letting go
feels much worse than the gain,
even when you know what the benefit is?
For you, letting go is going to be much more difficult
than it is for others.
Knowing this will create a shift in your perspective
so that you can be more understanding, patient,
and compassionate with yourself.

Why we keep paper

See if you can relate to one or more of the following. Rather than judging or criticizing yourself, use it as information to cultivate inner awareness.

We don't know what to do with it so we do nothing
(disempowering)

We can't make decisions
(procrastinating)

It takes our mind off of more important matters
(distracted)

We can't organize it right
(perfectionism)

We think it has importance
(overly attached)

We can't get it done fast enough
(impatient)

We don't want to feel the discomfort of letting it go
(avoidance)

We believe we might need it someday
(excuse)

We want to hold onto memories of happier times
(stuck in the past; overly sentimental)

We feel obligated to keep it
(guilt)

We believe that it can't be replaced
(fear)

This is why you won't miss what you toss out.
The memory is not in the piece of paper.
It's when you see the piece of paper
that the mind activates the memory.
If the paper is gone,
your mind can't trigger the memory.

The payoffs for holding on to paper

Being disorganized becomes our identity.

We can avoid dealing with paper as an excuse
to stay with the status quo.

Paper gives us something to focus on
so we don't have to face reality and
deal with life's challenges.

We use paper clutter to create unnecessary drama;
without the "tension", life can feel boring.

The "unfinished business" that comes with looking at
piles of paper can give us a sense of purpose,
i.e., it can make us feel needed and/or useful.

Humans hunger for familiarity because it feels safe.
As an example, when we lose weight and our body
begins to feel different, it feels unfamiliar.
If we are unable to sit with the emotional discomfort
of our body changing, then we may start
to quell the anxiety by overeating again.
We need to get used to feeling and looking different.
The same goes for reducing paper clutter.
As we begin to create more physical s p a c e,
our eye has to adjust to seeing things differently
or we may create more piles again.
Instead of sliding back into familiar territory,
give yourself time to adjust to the
newness that comes with change.

8 Consequences

Missing a critical deadline or
losing an important piece of paper
can be stressful, even embarrassing.

Unconsciously, holding on to clutter
is like dragging the weight of the past
with you wherever you go.

It can make you feel hopeless.

Too much paper leaves little room
for other interests.

It can affect your home's ability to function.

We are reluctant to have people over
because we feel shame.

Having to look for misplaced paper wastes time.

Clutter can even affect the way people treat you.

Clutter is defined as "a confused jumble of things."
It comes from the Middle English word "clotter"
which means to clot or coagulate.
Synonyms for coagulate are concrete, harden,
stiffen, thicken, lump.
No wonder we feel stuck.
Clutter is a burden physically,
emotionally, mentally, energetically and spiritually.

The nature of decluttering and getting organized is that
things will get worse before they get better.
This is because you are pulling things out of closets, desk
drawers, files, file cabinets, boxes, trunks and all the other
collection points in your house.
While this can be discouraging, don't give up.
It's part of the process.

7 things that block us from moving forward

It's one thing to know what your blocks are and another to do something about them. If you do nothing, nothing changes. If, for example, you need support and can't ask for it, explore your resistance so you can move forward.

Here are 7 blocks:

Not sure where to begin.

Don't know your next step.

Overwhelmed.

Fear of change.

Lack of motivation.

Being overly distracted.

Not enough time.

Can't ask for support.

D.I.E.T. stands for:
Desire • Intention • Eliminate • Tenacity

The Paper Diet's
four requirements for success:

First, there has to be a desire to change,
then a commitment to set a daily intention,
followed by the process of eliminating
what you don't want or need and, finally,
cultivating the tenacity to stay with it!

Getting started

Just because your paper piles are driving you crazy doesn't mean you have the desire or are even ready to make a change. Most of us would be willing to change if we could stay the same without the pain that comes with it. Getting started requires an action step and that can be as simple as deciding where to begin.

Once you have the **desire** and are ready to reduce your paper clutter, the first step is to set up your mail center. The root cause of the problem is not that the mail comes in every day but the inability to handle it consistently and with efficiency (see chapter on Mail Center).

An **intention** statement is a daily commitment that represents an action(s) that you will carry out for that day. This helps to break things down into manageable tasks (see chapter on Intention).

Eliminating paper is the requirement that will make you the most uncomfortable. The good news is that feeling emotionally, mentally and physically uncomfortable is a sign that you are making progress!

Tenacity is essential, especially if you are in the midst of a challenging project that can take a while to complete. Life doesn't happen in a straight line and neither does the process of purging paper. The key is to keep moving through the discomfort.
(see chapter on Hitting a plateau).

The Paper Diet's definition of insanity:
Keeping the same paper(s) year after year after year
with the hope that one day
you will wake up and
suddenly find a reason for keeping it.

The biggest excuse for keeping paper:
"I might need it someday."

You're holding a piece of paper and the thought of
letting it go is making you uncomfortable. So, you tell
yourself that you might need it someday. This is one
way to avoid feeling discomfort and postponing
the need to make a more informed decision.
It's the easy way out. Yes, you might need it someday
but 9 times out of 10, you won't.

The key is to sit with the discomfort, at least
long enough to give yourself time to ask
the following questions:

Can I get this information on the Internet?

Is there a specific circumstance where this information
would be useful again?

In what way is keeping this piece of paper
making my life better?

Does this piece of paper have a legal or tax purpose?

How hard would it be to replace this
piece of paper if I needed it?

What's the worse thing that will happen
if I toss it?

2 Suggestions for Setting a Daily Intention :

1.

When choosing your intention statement, avoid saying,
"I will try…",
"I might…",
or
"I would like to…".

It sounds stronger and makes you more accountable to
say,
"I will…",
"I am…",
or
"I choose to…"

2.

You may be able to do more than your intention.
However, if you don't accomplish your intention for that
day, avoid beating yourself up
(you have the world to do that for you).

Setting a daily intention

One of the most effective tools to promote forward
movement is to create a daily intention.
Basically, an intention is an aim
that guides your actions.

When you wake up each morning,
think about what you want to do for that day
to reduce paper clutter.

The most successful intentions include
a manageable task that is stated in the present tense,
then written down and posted where you will see it.

Here are some examples of intention statements:

"Today, I will clean out three files."

"Today, I choose to go through
one box of photographs."

"Today, I am setting up my mail center."

"Today, I will make a call to rectify the utility bill."

"Today, I am taking a break
from reducing paper clutter."
(so you don't feel guilty for taking a day off!)

To avoid paper piles,
this may be the most valuable habit that you can learn.
Remember the acronym for O.H.I.O.
"Only Handle It Once."
See if you can challenge yourself to act swiftly when it
comes into your home by putting every piece of paper
you touch in its proper place immediately.
Open your mail over the trash can or recycling bin.
File that receipt when you pull it out of the shopping bag.
Send a quick email to respond to that invitation.
Solutions like stuffing paper in drawers
are an easy way to reduce unsightly piles,
but it doesn't make the problem go away
(notice if avoidance is a pattern in other areas of your life).
Become aware of how many times
you pick up a piece of paper
and then put it down.

Creating a mail center

This may be the most important chapter in the book
because if you want to heal the wound,
you have to "stop the bleeding".
This requires that you set up a mail center or station
where sorting can be done in one central place.
Once this system is implemented,
your relationship with paper will improve dramatically.

Here's the big **F. A. T.** simple secret:
there are only three things you will do with paper:

File it
Act on it
Throw it away.

Here's the other big **F. A. T.** secret:
paper only goes in one of three places:

File cabinet or portable file box
Action folder
Trash can

In addition to a file cabinet, an action folder
and a trash can, you might also include:
Document shredder

Recycling bin
Additional "archive" file cabinet - inactive files

RED ACTION FOLDER - active file

Paper that requires an action step can be kept in a
red folder, tray or bin marked **"Action"** or **"Active"**.
Examples of action steps: scan, file, make a call,
wait for a response, verify (a receipt or bank statement),
fill out a form, delegate, sign, pay a bill, read, etc.

If you're holding a piece of paper that only requires a
couple of minutes to complete the action step,
do it right away. Every day or every couple of days,
go though your action file and see what needs to be
handled for that day. Once you have completed the
action step for that particular piece of paper,
either transfer to the inactive file or toss it out.

FILE CABINET - inactive files

This is where paper goes once you complete the action
step. Keep a separate folder for each category and title
them in a way that makes sense to you.
Examples: receipts, taxes, one file for each automobile
that will include everything to do with that car,
bills paid (for easy retrieval,
bind things like utility, insurance and
mortgage payments separately), medical records, etc.

A separate **ARCHIVE FILE** cabinet is optional and can
be kept in the attic, basement or a closet for storing
completed tax returns (use a different file for each year),
prior years' health records, warranties, etc.
These are files that don't need to be retrieved often.

3 TIPS:

1. Practice putting things where you will carry out the next action step. For example, if you read before falling asleep, stage your reading material and magazines next to your bed.

2. Once you set up your mail center and build in the daily habit of handing the incoming mail consistently, then as time allows, you can go back and tackle the existing piles, including boxes of photographs, memorabilia, stacks of magazines, receipts, files, and kids' art.

3. Remember, every piece of paper only goes in one of three places. For photographs, memorabilia and kids' art, a photo album or a decorative box becomes the "inactive" file. If you have a picture that you want to mail to someone, put it in your action folder. If you need to call a historical society that specializes in something you want to donate, put it in your action folder.

You probably wouldn't keep groceries in your bathroom
nor would you store toilet paper in the refrigerator.
Similarly, paper piles on the dining room table, floor or
kitchen counter prevent you from eating at a table,
walking around without stumbling, or having room
for your kitchen accessories and appliances.
If we don't set boundaries,
paper can easily take over our home,
often impacting those with whom we live.
Then it looks like we are making our stacks of paper
more important than the people in it.
Having said this, too much paper is not a home issue,
but a personal issue.

Boundaries

Boundaries are designed to make life more manageable and help you gain control. They also prevent you from feeling overwhelmed. Think of boundaries as a s p a c e allowance where you only have so much money and, therefore, need to stay within budget.

Here are 4 different kinds of boundaries:

Material boundaries:

Allow unread newspapers to remain in your home for a predetermined number of days before recycling.

Commit to tossing a preset number of pieces of paper every day.

Weed out your unused coupons monthly.

Keep your 5 favorite coffee mugs and give away the rest.

Time boundaries:

Set a timer and clear for 15 minutes
or eliminate 10 things every day
(a piece of paper counts as one thing).

Stay focused on your task for that day.

Physical boundaries:

A file cabinet, a bin on wheels, a manila folder,
a box of pictures, a trunk, a letter tray.
These are boundaries and, if they are overflowing
with paper, you have too much.

Visual boundaries:

To prevent immobilization, break it down into small
tasks, i.e., one box, one pile, one bookshelf at a time.

To help you keep track of everything and avoid
those messy looking refrigerators and post-it notes
everywhere, designate one place to record every
appointment, school event, sports practice
or social gathering.

The key to avoiding unsightly piles
is to designate an appropriate place
for each piece of paper.

It takes more effort to hold on
to something than it does to let it go.

The human body and mind are not designed
to handle more than one day at a time.
When clearing, always break it down.
Focus on one piece of paper,
one pile, one box, one surface area at a time.

Within those closets, trunks and boxes
are memories that can represent loss,
unresolved issues, postponed dreams.
We may avoid going through our pictures and memorabilia
because it reminds us of things that we feel guilty about,
that we don't want to face or even remember.
Yet, it may be the very thing that can
cleanse the drawers of the heart,
clear the cobwebs in the mind,
and heal the compartments of the soul.

Personal memorabilia

Most of us have a pantry, linen closet, or storage area for our stuff but no special place for things we have the most intimate relationship with - our memories. Rather than having them scattered all over the house, give yourself a much needed sense of order by taking the time to gather and organize them in one place.

Here is a list of possible categories:

Favorite childhood memories

Personal photographs

Special greeting cards, notes and letters

Journals

Scrapbooks

Artwork

Awards

School yearbooks

Diplomas

A specific trip or event with personal memorabilia including brochures and maps

3 TIPS:

1. For easy access, keep like things together. Take the time to make labels that are specific to the contents in the container. You may want to use clear containers because they show what's inside but you can also use keepsake boxes, attractive envelopes, baskets or trays.

2. If you don't have a closet to store your personal memories, then designate a trunk, cabinet or bookshelf unit.

3. You don't have to save everything, just your favorite memories, i.e., what you enjoyed doing, what you are most proud of, what your interests were at that stage in your life and what you accomplished.

If you don't know why
you are keeping something,
then let it go.

Avoid "decision density".
Every piece of paper that you pick up
requires that you make a decision.
This can be mentally and emotionally draining.
Stop a decluttering project just before you're ready
to because you'll need to straighten up, put things back
and still leave enough energy to accomplish
what needs to get done for that day.
It's a little like leaving a party
just before you're ready to go.
It takes time to say good-bye to the host,
acknowledge the people you see on
the way out the door, get to your car
and then make your way home.
It's knowing when to stop
that keeps you from burning out.

Organizing your photographs

Photographs can take up a lot of valuable storage space. When sorting, keep the best representative samples, whether it is an event, place and/or person.

Eliminate duplicates, duds and blurred pictures including those with people in them you don't know.

To reduce volume,
there are websites that offer digital scanning
and archival services for photographs.

Gather all of your photos in one place so that you not only see what you have but how much you have.

If available, use a large surface that will allow you to spread out and sort your photographs.

Divide your pictures by person, place, year or event.
Examples: vacation, graduation, pet,
wedding, child/person, hobby.

For easy access, place sorted photographs
in labeled folders.

6 TIPS:

1. Develop "tunnel vision". So that you don't get overwhelmed and become immobile, strive to focus on one stack, one shoebox, one envelope, one bin at a time.

2. Writing is an important part of history. As you sort, record what you know on the back of your photographs.

3. To stay on track, stop the project at a place where it's easy to come back to. If needed, make notes such as where you left off. Don't always rely on your memory.

4. To create more s p a c e and reduce volume, take old pictures out of their frames, especially if you don't plan on hanging them. Keep the frames you want and consign or give away the rest.

5. If you are having difficulty tossing pictures, send them to the people who are in them... or gift a recycled frame (#4) with an interesting photograph. You could also distribute your pictures at the next family reunion or holiday gathering which generates memories and sentimentality.

6. Use archival materials to protect your photographs. Store them away from bright light, extreme temperatures and fluctuating humidity. Remove photos from older magnetic photo albums and scrapbooks. Not only is the glue highly acidic but the plastic that covers your precious pictures is high in PVC which accelerates deterioration.

We think our identity is wrapped up
in what we keep,
but it isn't who we are.

Less photographs, better photographs.
If you only keep the best pictures,
they will not only seem significant and special,
but you will be more likely to enjoy
looking at them from time to time.
After all, isn't this the whole point
of saving them in the first place?

Avoid tempting yourself unnecessarily.
If you are a "paperaholic", don't open your junk mail.
It would be like wandering into a bar
if you are an alcoholic,
keeping sweets in the house
if you want to lose weight,
or going to the mall
if you are have a shopping addiction.

It's very freeing when you can resolve within yourself
that other people's memories
are not your memories
and that the four walls around your life
aren't going to collapse
when you toss the dried flower corsage
from your mother's high school prom.

Family papers and documents

Of all the paper we keep, family papers and documents are the most sentimental, making our emotional attachment to it perhaps the hardest, and deepest layer, to get through. There might be things like a manila folder with every record from your father's World War II days, old sepia photographs, your mother's calendar diaries, a postcard album from the early 19th century that belonged to your great aunt, your grandmother's handwritten list of all the places where she and your grandfather lived.

If feels like our ancestors, family members and relatives live on in those paper memories. For some, there's the added burden that we are betraying the person by letting go of their history. These are the memories that are usually kept in a trunk - stored out of sight - and just seeing them is another reminder that you've been dragging them around, maybe even for decades.

You might think if it's not visible, then it doesn't exist, but eventually you are going to have to deal with it. If you don't, these memories could easily end up in a landfill once you're gone.

So, what do you choose to keep?

A general rule of thumb is to keep papers that represent
a family member's legacy, that you are proud of, that
you like, that you will enjoy looking at from time to
time, that are interesting or have value to
members of your family.

If, however, you can't imagine you or anyone in
your family ever loving, wanting or
needing something in the foreseeable future,
then release them.

Some papers may have monetary or historic value
which can be sold. Letters, photos and cards
can be returned to the person who sent them
if they are still living. The rest can be recycled.

It's not just that you are creating s p a c e...
it's that your s p a c e is helping to create you.

6 TIPS:

1. There will be three categories when going through family papers: keep, toss, designate. Toss as you go and set aside the things you want to keep. What you don't want can be distributed to people you know, designating one pile for each person. Piles might include one for each sibling, your children, relatives of relatives, cousins, maybe even a friend.

2. In those designated piles are things like pictures, letters, documents, brochures and miscellaneous mementos. If someone is in a photograph, or their parents are in a photograph or you know they have a memory associated with that picture or piece of paper, it goes in their pile. If you think a certificate or memento is of interest to them or it will inspire a memory or their name is mentioned in a letter that someone wrote to another person, it also goes in their pile.

3. When you're done sorting, each pile of memories will go in a mailing envelope to be sent off to that person. In it will be a note stating that the contents are theirs to do with what they want, including any interesting facts about the enclosed mementos. Once they are in the mail, you won't believe how satisfying it is to share your family memories in this way. You feel good about giving and they are going to receive some "fun" mail.

4. Now that you have gone through the distribution process, set a boundary by choosing a set number of containers for the things you want to keep.

5. If you can't get everything in the limit that you have set, there's more culling to do. Toss those pictures of people and places you don't recognize, letters and cards with illegible writing and old restaurant menus with food stains. If it upsets you to see a picture of your grandfather looking emaciated after returning home from World War I, then let it go. Maybe you are keeping every Valentine's card that your father gave your mother. If so, keep the most charming two or three.

6. Be creative. If you have an abundance of old pictures taken of the house you grew up in, why not send them to the current owner? They, too, might enjoy something unexpected in the mail.

If brushing your teeth, taking a shower
and exercising regularly
are signs of good personal hygiene,
then good mental hygiene
is choosing to live with less clutter
and good emotional hygiene is being able to
handle the challenges and recover from any setbacks
that come with letting go.

Let's say you travel and leave your car
in the airport parking lot.
Unless you have a photographic memory,
most likely you will make a mental note
or write down the exact location of your vehicle.
Think of your files the same way.
By taking the time to put the papers
in the appropriate folder,
you won't have to go looking for them
because you know where they are...
... just like knowing where your car is
in the parking lot at the airport.

Important papers

There are as many opinions for how long to keep important papers as there are people you ask. Some say get rid of all but the most important papers. Others say keep everything. Ultimately you must decide based on your comfort level. For financial or tax-supporting documents, always check with a trusted advisor or your accountant first.

Here is a general rule of thumb for how long to keep important papers (in alphabetical order):

Appointment books/calendars
Determined by your personal preference. Consider if you going to keep them for memorabilia purposes or use for a reference.

ATM printouts
one month until you balance your checkbook

Bank statements
one year unless needed for tax purposes and then keep for 3 years

Auto repair receipts, maintenance records, title and registration
for as long as you own the vehicle

Bills paid (miscellaneous)
one year unless you need them for tax purposes

Cancelled checks
one year unless needed for tax purposes
and then keep for 3 years

Checkbook registers
one year unless needed for tax purposes
and then keep for 3 years

Contracts
hold while active

Credit card receipts
keep until you have reconciled
your monthly statement

Home improvement records
for as long as you own your home

Insurance policies
keep through the statue of limitations
in case of late claims

Medical bills
if you don't use them to itemize your taxes or for
insurance reimbursement, they can be disposed of
at the end of the year.
Otherwise, keep them for three years.

Paycheck stubs
keep to verify until you receive your W-2
at the end of the year

Property tax records - disputed bills
keep the bill until the dispute is resolved

Quarterly investment statements
keep until you get your annual statement

Records of pensions and
retirement plans
hold while active

Tax returns
Keep for 3 years, including supporting documentation
for the income and deductions that you claimed
including W-2's. The IRS can go back three years for
auditing purposes - civilly. Criminally, if they find
evidence of fraud or tax evasion,
they can go back further.

Utility Bills
one year, unless you're using these as a business
deduction in which case keep them for 3 years

Warranties
keep until you no longer own it

There is no free ride in life.
You can't buy the motivation required to effect change.
Therefore, it's quite unfortunate that by nature
human beings are lazy.
Hint: life doesn't come with a remote control;
you have to get up and move.
If you don't take action, nothing will change.

What to keep indefinitely

Birth certificate

Business license

Custody and adoption papers

Death certificate

Divorce decree(s)

Marriage license(s)

Military discharge papers

Pension plan documents

Records of paid mortgages

Social security card

Wills

Create a "smile pile" by putting all your favorite cards,
notes and letters in an attractive basket
for those days when you need a lift.

Remember, you only need one sentimental
piece of paper to keep the memory of someone alive.

It's one thing to keep a card, letter or note
that makes you feel sad because that person
has passed away or is no longer in your life.
But if it doesn't make you feel good
when you see it, why keep the reminder?

Cards, letters and notes

Cards, letters and notes can be sentimental jewels, but that doesn't mean you have to keep all of them. Even with e-cards, social media and email as a way to reach out, people still like to get and receive cards, hidden love notes around the house and letters in the mail.

Here are some creative ways to reduce, reuse and recycle those cards, letters and notes.

DISMANTLING CARDS
Think of each card as having three parts - the envelope, the inside sentiment and the card front.

First, by recycling the envelope, you are reducing the volume of paper by half.

Second, cut out handwritten sentiments from the inside of cards which can be kept in a journal, photo album or file.

Third, reuse the card fronts to make your own greeting cards. Purchase a box of blank white, off-white or colored cards with envelopes. Tear off the front of the used card, crop it to fit, and glue it to the front of the new blank card.

You can also do this with holiday cards, reusing the fronts of this year's cards and use them to make homemade cards for next year.

Other creative ways to reuse card tops:

Repurpose them into postcards.
On the back of the card, draw a line down the center,
write a sentiment on the left side,
address the right side and put a stamp on it.

Recycle card fronts to embellish photo albums and
scrapbooks or to use as bookmarks.

Use for table place cards.
Or, to make a gift tag, punch a hole in the corner
and thread a piece of string or ribbon through it.

If you have children, save card fronts
for art and craft projects or
for decorating their bedrooms.

Donate card tops to summer camp organizations.
Some will repurpose your card tops
into new cards that are then sold
to raise funds for the organization.

For cards that you aren't going to dismantle,
separate them into piles - one for each person
who gave it to you. Use a separate file folder,
labelled with their name and store them away.

LETTERS AND NOTES

Special notes and letters can be put in a picture frame.

Scan letters and notes and create folders on your computer by subject, person or year.

You might consider returning old letters and cards to those who sent them. Getting them back will be like receiving a time capsule.

If something has a special memory associated with it, take a photo so you don't have to keep the piece of paper.

When a family member passes away, be very careful about bringing their paper memories into your home especially if you don't have time or aren't interested in doing anything with them. Once something enters your home, it's three times harder to get it out.

If you want to be a good role model for kids,
walk the talk.
Let them see that you are sorting through your own stuff
on a regular basis.
When decluttering, start when they are young.
Remind them that there are things that we hold onto
and there are things that we let go of.

Kids' school papers and artwork

Most parents are drowning under the deluge of papers
that their kids bring home from school.

With daily backpacks unloading art work, sports
schedules, rosters and meeting notices, it doesn't take
long before the piles are creating havoc.

Separate into five piles:
Action file, keep for now, mail, frame, trash/recycle

ACTION FILE
Anything that needs your attention goes into
your red action file or handle it right away,
i.e., filling and/or signing a form, respond to an
invitation, or marking a date on your calendar.

KEEP FOR NOW
For each child, you will need a large container, bin or
basket. Throughout the school year, you will collect
things like school papers, special awards, self portraits,
school pictures, birthday cards,
graded homework, report cards, artwork,
invitations, ribbons, letters and cards.

MAIL
Tossing kids' artwork can be unbearable, but you can't keep everything either. One solution is to mail things to others. Decide with your child who to send their artwork to - grandparents, aunts and uncles, godparents, former teachers or baby-sitters. Have your child personalize it by adding a note and/or signing their name on the back.

FRAME
Who doesn't like seeing their artwork on the wall? Hanging it makes kids feel special and also sends a message that you appreciate their work.

TRASH/RECYCLE
Anything that needed an immediate response but you have taken care of. Items that you know won't be needed for future reference. Insignificant homework assignments and graded papers.

4 TIPS:

1. Avoid letting your kids dump their backpacks or school bags on the floor or counter when they come home. Have them unload their things and help you sort through the papers for that day.

2. While school work and art projects can never be replaced once they are tossed, they can be photographed or scanned and turned into a photo book. Make an extra copy or two to give as gifts for their grandparents.

3. One way to work with boundaries is to keep only what will go in a 3 ring binder. If your child only drew birds for a while, help them to keep the best two or three representative samples.

4. As a fun summer project* with your kids, go through their container for the school year and create a portfolio. Use this opportunity to validate their school work and make comments. A project such as this is not only creative, but teaches them how to take care of and preserve their things. They will learn how to set boundaries by keeping just enough to give them an idea of what they accomplished that year. You can help them make decisions by discerning what to give away and what to keep such as milestones, things that they are proud of, paper that represents their best work and that is meaningful to them.

Supplies needed for the project:

3 ring binder

Regular plastic sheet protectors -
(to protect everything you want to keep)

Tab divider sheets -
(for naming different categories and subjects)

Plastic bin, magazine folder or other container -
(for storage of the 3 ring binder which can be labeled
with their name and age or year.
Bigger items that don't fit in the sheet protectors
can also go in the container)

*you could enlist their grandparents
to do the project with them.*

You will feel like you've accomplished more
if you tackle a single project and follow it
through from beginning to end.
You can jump from place to place,
but you won't see as much progress.
If you have A.D.D. or A.D.H.D.,
staying on course will be a real challenge.
As soon as you start to stray from what you are doing,
stop yourself and say, "No, I am working on this right now."
Be persistent. You might need to say this
over and over and over.

The spiritual life is about letting go,
so share the bounty.
A single book that you give away could inspire,
even change the life of another person.

Books

Most of us, on an subconscious level, strongly identify
with our books so letting them go can feel like we are
giving away our stockpile of knowledge.
They also carry memories of better times,
fueling our nostalgic side. But energetically,
holding onto books that we no longer need or want
can prevent us from creating new ideas
and ways of thinking to come into our life.

At the very least, see if you can let go of one book
for every new one you bring home.

To begin, go through your home and
gather all your books in one place.

Sort them into six piles:
keep, donate, discard, gift, sell or swap.

Discard books that are trashed,
have visible signs of mildew or that smell musty.

Donate books to schools, used bookstores, thrift shops,
senior centers, prisons or hospitals.

If you have bookshelves, arrange the books you want to
keep by size, subject, favorite genre, author,
signed volumes, etc. To create a more balanced look,
store the heaviest books on the bottom shelf.
Gift used books in good condition.

If you don't want to micro-manage the fate of each
book, take them all to one donation center or book
depository and trust that the Universe
will get them to the right people.

Sell your books online, to consignment shops
or, for rare books, search the internet for antique
book appraisers/dealers.

No more excuses that you don't have enough time.

We always find time for the things that are important.

Every person on this planet has the exact same number
of hours each day, the same number that are given to
those who are able to accomplish four times as much
as most of us. If purging paper matters to you,
then it becomes a commitment issue, not a time issue.

3 TIPS:

1. Set boundaries. Keep your 5 favorite cookbooks and give away the rest. Similarly, if you've outgrown a collection of children's books or books on European travel because they longer hold the same interest, keep the most prized one.

2. Questions to ask yourself:

   Will I ever read or look through this book again?

   Does this book reflect my interests now?

   Has it served its purpose?

   Does it carry a positive memory?

   Can I access the information online?

3. Remember that almost everything can be referenced online, including all the facts and data found in those heavy textbooks that take up so much valuable s p a c e.

Minimize tolerations.
Tolerations are anything that drains your energy,
i.e., the mere sight of those paper piles
when you walk into a room,
tripping over a stack of magazines or newspapers,
not being able to find something,
moving boxes of old papers from place to place.

It takes time to realize that most paper isn't
as important as it seemed when you first saw it.
It also takes time to realize that it isn't really
adding any value to your life either.
This is what makes it important to
periodically purge paper.

Magazines

Magical thinking is believing we will have time to read everything that comes into our home. Most of us won't live long enough to keep up with the amount of information that bombards us on a daily basis. If you tend to hoard magazines, it may be a fear that you are going to miss out on some important piece of information if you throw it out.
You won't.
And you won't miss it once it's gone.

The quick approach to letting go:
Gather all your magazines, including the ones in the basement, attic and garage, and pack them up for recycling.
Then, vow to cancel any subscriptions that you no longer enjoy reading or want.

The slower approach to letting go:
Tear interesting articles out of magazines to read later. Then dispose of the magazine to reduce volume. Shred magazine pages and use as filler when shipping boxes. Or, keep them for craft projects such as collages, decoupage and memory boards. Magazines can be a valuable teaching tool when donated to literacy programs. Schools may also take them for art projects.

5 TIPS:

1. Consider donating magazines that you've read to your local gym, waiting rooms, nursing homes, homeless shelters, laundromats and senior centers.

2. Pass magazines along to family, friends, co-workers, and neighbors... or share subscriptions.

3. It's hard to catch up once you get behind, so when a new magazine comes in, let go of the old one. If you can't do that, pull the articles that you haven't had time to read and put them in a folder. Stage the folder by door where it can then go into your car to be taken to appointments to make better use of wait time. Or, take the folder with you on your next vacation when you have more time to catch up.

4. If you have a collection of vintage magazines, store each one in an archival plastic sleeve (available online or at your local art supply store). Put each sleeve inside a water resistance box, organize according to date or category, and store in a cool, dry location to avoid mold and mildew. Avoid keeping them in areas that are subject to extreme heat such as attics or garages. Note that light can cause colors to fade.

5. Use the recycling bin for catalogs, magazines and newspapers. Tear off the mailing label or purchase a black out pen.

It's not natural for our shoulders to ache.
Notice if you have chronic tension in that area.
If so, you may be carrying around too many "shoulds"
in your life... "I should be keeping this magazine
(because there's something important that I need to know),
I should be keeping this family document
(because my children may want it someday)."
Note that the word "should" is in the word "shoulder".

Nineteen billion catalogs are mailed out
to American homes each year.
The production of these catalogs
requires 53 million trees, 53 billion gallons of water and
emits 5.2 million tons of carbon dioxide.

If you don't want to risk being pestered by having your
name and contact information added to a marketing list,
avoid subscribing to things, filling out warranty cards
and credit card applications, catalog shopping, making
donations, or entering a contest.

Catalogs

Month after month, the raft of catalogs floods your mailbox. After a while, it can be annoying to receive so many, especially if you have lost interest in a certain company's products or you only bought one thing from them.

Granted, catalogs can be fun, relaxing and entertaining to browse through, but the bigger problem is that many are filled with items that you never even knew existed.

If you are prone to shopping for things you don't need, recycle them as soon as they arrive.

Contact the company and ask them to stop having their catalogs sent to you. While they may still sell your name, at least you are making the effort to reduce volume.

You can also Google
"how to unsubscribe from mail catalogs."

Ask yourself,
"What one thing could I do today
that would make my life with paper
a little better tomorrow?"

Acronyms for D.I.E.T.:
Do I Eliminate This?
Does It Ease Tension?
Do I Enjoy This?

Receipts

Paper receipts can be found almost anywhere
without a plan for managing them -
in our wallets, hidden in the glove compartment
of the car, stuffed in junk drawers,
wedged between sofa cushions,
tucked between the pages of books.
All because we probably don't know
how to organize them or
don't have the time or
there are too many to deal with.

Whatever the reason,
make the effort.

Once you give up receipt mania and
get them under control,
the day-to-day maintenance is easy.

Start with today's receipts.
Then, when you have time to work
in one or two hour increments,
sort and organize the ones you are going to keep.

10 TIPS:

1. Each day's receipts can go right into your red "action" folder (see *Creating a mail center,* page 17). The action step is to file them.

2. Create an inactive file folder marked "Receipts". For receipts from stores where you shop frequently, create a sub-category to put in the main receipt file (sort folders alphabetically by sub-category). However, if you have a receipt for tax purposes, then file it in your current tax file. Similarly, if you have a receipt or warranty card for a household item, put it in a file marked "Household".

   Note: *If your current filing system for paper is working, then don't fix it.*

3. If you don't have a lot of receipts, you could paperclip the current year's receipts together by month and put them in your receipt file.

4. When you are ready to go back and organize your past receipts, gather them all into one pile. Start at the top and vow to handle each receipt only once (see *O.H.I.O.,* page 16). Toss receipts that are obviously outdated or way past their return date, personal expenses that you can't deduct from your taxes and gas receipts if you've paid with credit and reconciled the charge.

5. Receipts for utilities, rent, and anything associated with deductions and credits claimed on your tax return should be kept for a year.

6. Credit card receipts can be destroyed once you have verified purchases or reconciled your monthly statement.

7. Keep a grocery receipt if you bought produce and aren't sure of its quality or you bought a new item and found that you didn't like it. For clothes, keep receipts for the length of the return period or until you wear it (typically you can't make a return once the tags have been removed and it has been worn). For owners manuals and big household items, keep the receipts for the life of the warranty or until you no longer own them.

8. Sometimes, receipts are so faded that they are unreadable. Or, it's hard to figure out or remember what you bought by looking at the receipt. Save time by writing relevant information on the receipt before you file it. If you get audited, and you have expenses for entertaining clients, the IRS will want to know their name, what was discussed, the date, and the name of the restaurant or event. Don't commit to memory. Write the information on a piece of paper and staple it to the receipt.

9. If you like to track all of your expenses, keep an envelope in your red "action folder" where you can temporarily hold that week's receipts until you evaluate, add and record them.

10. Receipts can also be organized digitally or scanned and stored on your personal computer.

Sometimes, when you keep something
because you might need it for legal or medical reasons,
it can actually attract a situation into your life
that you may not want.

Avoid "pickup-itis".
When you're out in public, break the habit
of compulsively grabbing pamphlets, brochures,
business cards and advertisement flyers -
or taking stuff that other people thrust into your hands -
especially if you have little or no interest
in doing anything with them.
While they are "free, it will cost you time.
You still have to do something with it,
even if it only takes five seconds.

Miscellaneous paper

We may be edging toward a paperless world but phone books, business cards, coupons, vouchers and mailers along with a penchant for clipping articles and recipes from newspapers and magazines do not appear to be disappearing anytime soon.

BUSINESS CARDS

Business cards are small enough to end up anywhere and everywhere until we need one and can't find it.

They are best kept in one place, whether it means transferring their contact information to your smartphone or keeping them in a small box or organized in a rolodex-type business card file. When weeding through your current stack of business cards, be ruthless. Why keep one if you don't recognize the person or the company and don't need their services?

COUPONS

If you are going to take the time to cut coupons or keep coupon books, then use them. They are of little use if you keep them at home so stage them where they are accessible when you need them - in your wallet or the glove compartment of your car.

NEWSPAPER ARTICLES

Sort into 3 piles: toss, send to people who might enjoy reading the article and keep. Those that you want to keep can be kept in a file, scanned into the computer, or added to your scrapbooks (either photocopy the article or buy a spray product that neutralizes the acid in the paper and stops it from becoming yellow and brittle).

PHONE BOOKS

These are real s p a c e hogs and, unless you are without a computer, there is little reason to keep them.

Most contact information can be found online.

To stop receiving phone books, the Yellow Pages Association lists the publishers in your area with a phone number to call.

RECIPE CLIPPINGS

Like the mail, magazines and newspapers keep coming and, in them, are more recipes for you to clip and try out. You don't have to get rid of them all but if you want to reduce piles, always set boundaries. Go through and weed your old stack and keep 10. When you clip a new one, let go of an old one. If you accidentally toss a recipe and decide later that you want to make it, you can find something similar online.

It's really true...
out of sight, out of mind.

We don't accumulate paper all at once,
yet we expect it to be undone in a week.
Piles add up gradually, one piece at a time,
sometimes over long periods.
Remember this: it will prevent you from giving up.

Scanning

Scanning is an easy way to lighten your load
while keeping your paper memories alive.
Basically, scanning converts hard copy documents
to digital images that can then be
transferred to a computer.

We would all like to be paper free for easier
accessibility and to save s p a c e,
but scanning takes time and effort
especially if you have large amount of stuff.
You will first need to remove paperclips, staples,
and picture frames if you are scanning photographs.
Add to that the time it will take to index the documents
once they are scanned so you can find them
on your computer.

It's important to know why you are saving something.
Perhaps the most important question is this:

**Would it be catastrophic if this piece of paper
were lost forever? If so, scan it.**

3 TIPS:

1. Once you have a scanner hooked up to your computer, almost any paper can be scanned - old letters, newspaper clips (like wedding announcements), greeting cards, report cards, children's art, and more.

2. Documents that are not scannable: if they are larger than the surface of the scanner, if the are not flat, or need to contain certain security features like the special reflective material in checks.

3. If you have a lot of documents and paper to be scanned, take them to a copy center.

The Paper Diet Limerick:

While you aren't beguiled,
you're still on trial
to dial back those files
and miles of piles
with style and a smile.

Life is about gain and loss.
With every exhale, we let go.
With every inhale,
we are in the next, new moment of our life.
When you let go of a piece of paper,
begin to acknowledge the gain
(to jog your mind, see chapter on
10 good reasons to let go of paper).

Getting rid of paper
means you are making decisions.
If you aren't making decisions,
then you're in limbo.
Being in limbo is a subtle form of stress.

Shredding

Shredding is a simple solution if you are looking for a safe and secure way to protect your privacy, prevent identity theft and avoid falling victim to scams. The other benefit is that shredding companies will recycle whatever documents they've shredded which is better for the environment than dumping it into a landfill. Depending on how much you have, it can also reduce storage costs when you shred as much as possible.

Here is a list of things to shred:

Anything with your address, signature or social security number

Old papers that include your birthdate

Account numbers

Passwords and pin numbers

Deposit slips and credit card receipts
(after you verify your monthly statement)

Old medical and insurance bills

Pre-approved credit card applications

Expired I.D.'s such as driver's licenses, green cards and passports

Canceled checks that you don't need for tax purposes

4 TIPS:

1. When buying a shredder, consider how much paper you have and how much time you want to spend shredding. Some shredders do one sheet at a time while more expensive models can handle 10 - 12.

2. If you have a large volume of paper, such as boxes of family documents, tax records and expired files, hire someone to come to your home. They will shred everything on the truck right in front of you or take it off-site for shredding.

3. Go online to find the best rates for on-site or off-site shredding services. If you own a business, some companies will offer a "frequent shredder" card or discount if you sign up for regular monthly or bimonthly shredding. With bigger machines to do the work, shredding goes much faster than doing it yourself.

4. Some areas offer free shredding on certain days. Google the name of your town/tree shredding to find out what your options are.

Even though we know
that completing a project is satisfying,
we may choose to stall
in order to slow down our progress.
It might mean that you need to give yourself time
to integrate the changes.
Or, it could mean that bringing closure or
finishing projects is hard for you.

In the plateau phase,
avoid getting discouraged.
Things can shift in the next breath.
You will get through it.
Trust this.

Hitting a plateau

Once the initial enthusiasm and accomplishment wears off, many of us hit the middle, or plateau, phase.

Plateaus are designed to test your resolve, to see how serious you really are about having what you say you want. But it's also the perfect time to look back and see how far you've come.

Sometimes, lack of motivation can mean that we need a break. The process of letting go sounds simple but simple is not always easy. If it were, we would all be doing it.

Often, the cause is the "ongoingness" of everyday life that leaves us with little or no time and energy to keep going. Obstacles can cause us to temporarily give up, too. Maybe we're irritated at ourselves because we need support and don't know how to ask for it.

No human undertaking is linear and they all take time. It's the inevitable ebb and flow of life... progress followed by stagnation followed by bursts of more progress.

Fighting it will only make things worse. Instead, step into the flow and ride the wave.

Live "organically"... allow rather than force.

5 TIPS:

1. Notice where you might be slacking. Are you setting your intention every morning?

2. Ask yourself, "What is my next step?" If it's picking a date to tackle a particularly difficult file or box of papers, block out time on your calendar (active) which is more productive than thinking about it (passive). Even if you aren't able to follow through on that date, it will give you a boost to take that action step by marking your calendar.

3. Are you taking care of your body, i.e., getting enough sleep, eating well and exercising with regularity? Notice if your thoughts about reducing paper clutter reflect the way you think about yourself. All of this can affect your progress.

4. Be gentle on yourself. Adjust your expectations. Eliminate the word "should" from your vocabulary.

   Recognize your limitations. Explore ways to get support if that's what you need.

5. Plateaus are a good time for reflection which is part of the process anyway. Sometimes, it helps to walk away and get out in nature in order to move the energy in the mind and body. This can also put things in perspective.

One way to build in an old habit is
to pair it with a new habit.
While you are enjoying an
afternoon cup of tea,
sort through a stack of magazines
or pile of mail...
or go through a box of photos
while you're watching television.

Doing something for fifteen minutes a day
has a greater impact than eight hours all at once
(and then not doing anything for a while).
It's the consistent building in of a daily habit
that generates results.

8 quick tips to reduce paper clutter

1. Consistency builds a habit, so handle your incoming mail everyday.

2. Open your mail over the trash. This reduces outer envelopes, junk mailings, unwanted coupons, and any other paper clutter.

3. Create a mail center to get organized and prevent piles.

4. When possible, handle things as soon as they come through the door, especially it if only requires a couple of minutes to complete an action step. Then you can toss that piece of paper.

5. Practice the one in, one out guideline. When the new catalog, newspaper or magazine comes in, recycle the old one.

6. Evaluate your subscriptions. Keep only the ones that you love and read on a regular basis.

7. To maintain balance, purge your paper files yearly (or every time the seasons change) to create room for the next year's avalanche of paper.

8. Sign up to receive statements and bills electronically. Pay your bills online. Create a digital filing system by scanning your files and documents. You can then shred the documents, unless there is a reason you need to keep the original, ex: a birth certificate.

Take a moment to notice
what you do consistently in your life.
Whether it's taking care of yourself
or complaining too much
or paying your bills on time
or eating foods that make you feel lethargic.
Because it's what you do consistently
that defines the quality of your life.

Paper needs to earn a right
to take up s p a c e in your home.
It sucks precious time and energy to file it,
move it from place to place,
look through it, scan it,
keep track of it, store it, and/or shred it.

6 ways to reduce paper usage

1. When grocery shopping, keep reusable bags in your car. Post a note on your dashboard until you are in the habit of remembering to take them into the store.

2. Take the necessary steps to reduce unwanted mail. While this requires the most time, it has the biggest impact.

3. Consume consciously; packaging makes up 30% of the weight and 50% of trash by volume.

4. Be frugal when it comes to magazines and newspaper subscriptions.

5. If you are not an ebook reader, get books from the library, buy them used, or share with friends.

6. Set up your computer to automatically print two-sided. Proofread your work carefully before hitting the print button.

Remember as a kid when you had a cut
and it was time to take the band-aid off?
You either took it off slowly,
taking the torturous route
or you ripped it off,
causing a quick, short burst of pain.

The same idea applies
when reducing old boxes of paper.
Let's say you have a catchall box
that includes things like gas and grocery store receipts,
unopened junk mail and other miscellaneous paper.
For months, maybe even years,
you've been keeping this box.
You haven't opened it because
there is nothing in it that you've missed or needed.
You can either take the box and, with great bravery,
toss the whole thing or open it and
painstakingly go through each piece of paper.

Which will you choose?
By the way, how did you remove that
band-aid when you were a kid?

Compiling an emergency file

This is a file that will be much appreciated by the person who is handling your affairs after you die (in which case you will tell him/her where to find the file).

Also, it will be easy to grab if you ever need to evacuate your home in a hurry. Save yourself a big headache and take the time to put together a file with your most important papers.
You will want to update it every year.

Here is a list in alphabetical order:

A list of all your passwords

Bank account and
credit card account numbers

Birth certificate

Copies of your driver's license and
other identification cards

Copies of lifesaving prescriptions

Emergency contact information
(for doctors, family, insurance agents,
doctors, etc.)

Marriage certificates, divorce
or change of name decree

Miscellaneous legal documents

Passport

Retirement savings and investment records
(including contact information
of your financial advisor)

Social security card

Tax returns - last 3 years

Title to your car

Utility account numbers

Will

What if you are finally organized and no longer
have to scramble around to find things.
You know it's what you've been wanting,
what you've worked so hard for,
but you feel uncomfortable because it's too easy.
You're used to the hassle, to life being difficult,
and now the struggle is over.
Avoid falling back into old habits.
You're birthing a new life!

About the Author

Kater's passion for simplicity can be traced back to 1974 when she spent six months living off the land in Colorado. Now armed with valuable knowledge and experience, she offers unique insights and wisdom that encourage others to release the struggle that comes with excess. This empowers us to live a more balanced, less encumbered life.

Kater's offerings also include teaching yoga, writing inspirational articles, professional organizing, staging homes to sell and leading workshops.

She lives near Annapolis, Maryland where all of her work is based on guiding others to live better.